ALEXANDER-GRACE EDUCATION

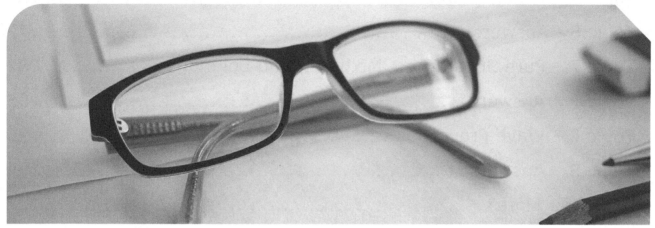

CONTENTS

ALEXANDER-GRACE EDUCATION

Understanding the MAP Tests

The NWEA MAP (Measures of Academic Progress) test is an adaptive assessment that is designed to measure student growth and progress in a variety of subject areas. The test is taken by millions of students across the United States and is widely used by educators to help inform instruction and measure student outcomes. The NWEA MAP test is administered online and provides immediate feedback on student performance, allowing teachers to adjust their teaching strategies and provide targeted support to individual students.

The NWEA MAP test is unique in that it is adaptive, which means that the difficulty of the questions adjusts based on the student's responses. This allows the test to be more personalized to each student's abilities and provides a more accurate measure of their knowledge and skills. The test covers a range of subject areas, including mathematics, reading, language usage, and science, and is administered multiple times throughout the school year. This allows teachers to track student progress and growth over time and make data-driven decisions to improve student outcomes.

Purpose and Benefits of MAP Testing

The primary purpose of the MAP Test is to provide valuable insights into a student's learning and academic progress. By offering a detailed analysis of a student's performance in reading, language usage, mathematics, and science, the test helps teachers tailor their instruction to meet individual needs. The MAP Test also serves as a benchmarking tool, allowing schools and districts to compare their students' performance with national norms and other local institutions.

This data-driven approach enables educators to make informed decisions about curriculum, instructional methods, and resource allocation, ultimately leading to improved student outcomes. Additionally, the MAP Test can help identify gifted students who may benefit from advanced or accelerated programs, as well as students who may require additional support or interventions.

Test Format and Content

The MAP Test is divided into four primary content areas: reading, language usage, mathematics, and science. Each section consists of multiple-choice questions that cover various topics and skills within the respective subject. The test is untimed, allowing students to work at their own pace and ensuring a lower level of test anxiety. The computer-adaptive nature of the MAP Test ensures that the difficulty of questions adjusts based on a student's performance, making it suitable for students of all ability levels. As a result, the MAP Test not only evaluates a student's mastery of grade-level content but also assesses their readiness for more advanced material.

Adaptive Testing and Scoring System

One of the unique aspects of the MAP Test is its adaptive testing system. As students answer questions, the test adjusts the difficulty of subsequent questions based on their performance. This adaptive nature allows the test to home in on a student's true ability level, providing more accurate and meaningful results. The MAP Test uses a RIT (Rasch Unit) scale to measure student achievement, which is an equal-interval scale that allows for easy comparison of scores across grade levels and subjects. This scoring system allows educators and parents to track a student's growth over time, making it an invaluable tool for understanding academic progress and setting individualized learning goals.

Preparing for Success on the MAP Test

Effective preparation for the MAP Test involves a combination of understanding the test format, mastering content knowledge, and developing test-taking strategies. This test prep book is designed to provide students with comprehensive guidance on each content area, offering targeted instruction and practice questions to build confidence and ensure success. Additionally, the book includes test-taking tips and strategies to help students approach the test with a calm and focused mindset. By working through this book and dedicating time to consistent practice, students will be well-equipped to excel on the MAP Test and achieve their academic goals.

Note that, since there is no cap to the level that a student can work to in preparation for this test, there is no 'completion' of content, as students can simply do questions from grades above in preparation. It should be noted that students are not expected to work far above grade level to succeed in this test, as consistent correct answers are more relevant.

What Is Contained Within this Book?

Within this book you will find 320 questions based off content which would be found within the MAP test your student will take. The content found in this book will be the equivalent of grade 5 level. Note that since this test is adaptive, some students may benefit by looking at several grade levels of content, not just their own.

At the end of the book will contain answers alongside explanations. It is recommended to look and check your answers thoroughly in regular intervals to make sure you improve as similar questions come up.

Topic 1 - Chemical Reactions

1.1) What is a chemical reaction?

☐ Mixing two liquids together

☐ A change where new substances are formed

☐ Freezing a liquid

☐ Heating an object

1.2) What is needed to start a chemical reaction?

☐ Water

☐ Light

☐ A catalyst

☐ Heat

1.3) What is the term for a substance that speeds up a chemical reaction?

☐ Inhibitor

☐ Catalyst

☐ Solution

☐ Reactant

1.4) What is produced when an acid reacts with a base?

□ Water and a salt

□ Gas

□ Another acid

□ Sugar

1.5) What do you call substances that are used up in a chemical reaction?

□ Products

□ Reactants

□ Catalysts

□ Solutions

1.6) What is the process called when a iron reacts with oxygen and water?

□ Melting

□ Dissolving

□ Rusting

□ Burning

1.7) What type of reaction releases energy in the form of heat or light?

□ Exothermic reaction

□ Endothermic reaction

□ Physical reaction

□ Neutralization

1.8) What do we call a change that forms new substances?

☐ Physical change

☐ Chemical change

☐ State change

☐ Reversible change

1.9) What gas is commonly produced when an acid reacts with a metal?

☐ Oxygen

☐ Carbon dioxide

☐ Hydrogen

☐ Nitrogen

1.10) What happens to the atoms in a chemical reaction?

☐ They disappear

☐ They change into new atoms

☐ They rearrange to form new substances

☐ They stay the same

1.11) What is a 'reactant' in a chemical reaction?

☐ A product formed

☐ A substance that is used up

☐ A tool used in the lab

☐ A type of catalyst

1.12) What does 'pH' measure in a substance?

□ Weight

□ Temperature

□ Acidity or basicity

□ Volume

1.13) What is created when an acid and a base neutralize each other?

□ Another acid

□ Another base

□ A neutral substance

□ Water

1.14) What is rusting an example of?

□ Physical change

□ Chemical change

□ State change

□ Reversible change

1.15) Which is a sign that a chemical reaction has taken place?

□ Change in color

□ Change in size

□ Change in shape

□ Change in texture

1.16) What type of chemical reaction absorbs energy?

□ Exothermic reaction

□ Endothermic reaction

□ Neutralization

□ Oxidation

1.17) What happens in a combustion reaction?

□ A substance burns in oxygen

□ A metal rusts

□ A liquid freezes

□ A gas condenses

1.18) What is a solution in chemistry?

□ A mixture where substances are spread out evenly

□ A solid substance

□ A type of chemical reaction

□ A tool used in the lab

1.19) What is the term for when a gas turns into a liquid?

□ Evaporation

□ Sublimation

□ Condensation

□ Deposition

1.20) What are the new substances formed in a chemical reaction called?

☐ Reactants

☐ Catalysts

☐ Solutions

☐ Products

1.21) What happens in a displacement reaction?

☐ A solid is formed

☐ One element replaces another

☐ Two liquids mix

☐ A gas is released

1.22) What is the name of the energy stored in chemical bonds?

☐ Kinetic energy

☐ Potential energy

☐ Thermal energy

☐ Mechanical energy

1.23) What do we call the point in a reaction where reactants are turned into products?

☐ End point

☐ Mid point

☐ Transition point

☐ Reaction point

1.24) What is a 'precipitate' in a chemical reaction?

☐ A gas that forms

☐ A solid that forms

☐ A liquid that forms

☐ A color change

1.25) What is an indicator in chemistry?

☐ A tool to measure volume

☐ A substance that changes color in different pH

☐ A type of chemical reaction

☐ A catalyst

1.26) What is the name of the process where plants convert sunlight into energy?

☐ Photosynthesis

☐ Respiration

☐ Combustion

☐ Evaporation

1.27) Which gas is essential for combustion to occur?

☐ Hydrogen

☐ Oxygen

☐ Nitrogen

☐ Carbon dioxide

1.28) What is it called when two or more substances are mixed and no new substance is formed?

☐ Chemical reaction

☐ Physical change

☐ Catalytic reaction

☐ Endothermic reaction

1.29) What type of reaction happens when a substance combines with oxygen, releasing energy?

☐ Oxidation

☐ Reduction

☐ Neutralization

☐ Precipitation

1.30) What happens in an oxidation reaction?

☐ A substance loses oxygen

☐ A substance gains oxygen

☐ A substance loses electrons

☐ A substance gains hydrogen

1.31) What is it called when energy is taken in during a chemical reaction?

☐ Exothermic reaction

☐ Endothermic reaction

☐ Catalytic reaction

☐ Oxidation reaction

1.32) Which is not a sign of a chemical reaction?

☐ Color change

☐ Temperature change

☐ Shape change

☐ Gas production

1.33) What type of reaction occurs when acids and bases react together?

☐ Combustion

☐ Neutralization

☐ Oxidation

☐ Precipitation

1.34) What is the law that states mass is conserved in a chemical reaction?

☐ Law of Definite Proportions

☐ Law of Conservation of Mass

☐ Law of Multiple Proportions

☐ Law of Chemical Reactions

1.35) What do you call a substance that slows down a chemical reaction?

☐ Catalyst

☐ Inhibitor

☐ Accelerator

☐ Reactant

1.36) What is the primary difference between a physical change and a chemical change?

☐ Physical changes are reversible

☐ Chemical changes create new substances

☐ Physical changes need energy

☐ Chemical changes are faster

1.37) What is the term for a reaction that gives off heat?

☐ Exothermic reaction

☐ Endothermic reaction

☐ Thermal reaction

☐ Kinetic reaction

1.38) What happens to atoms in a chemical reaction?

☐ They are destroyed

☐ They change into other atoms

☐ They are rearranged

☐ They disappear

1.39) What is a compound?

☐ A mixture of two elements

☐ A pure element

☐ A substance made of two or more elements chemically combined

☐ A type of chemical reaction

1.40) What are the names of all the different types of atom?

☐ Atomic Identity

☐ Element

☐ Molecule

☐ Particle

Topic 1 – Answers

Question Number	Answer	Explanation
1.1	A change where new substances are formed	A chemical reaction involves a change where new substances with different properties are formed.
1.2	A catalyst	A catalyst is often needed to start or speed up a chemical reaction.
1.3	Catalyst	A catalyst speeds up a chemical reaction without being consumed in the process.
1.4	Water and a salt	An acid-base reaction typically produces water and a salt.
1.5	Reactants	Reactants are substances that are used up in a chemical reaction to form products.
1.6	Rusting	Iron reacts with oxygen and water in a process called rusting, which is a chemical change.
1.7	Exothermic reaction	An exothermic reaction releases energy, often in the form of heat or light.
1.8	Chemical change	A chemical change is a process that results in the formation of new substances.
1.9	Hydrogen	When an acid reacts with a metal, hydrogen gas is commonly produced.
1.10	They rearrange to form new substances	In a chemical reaction, atoms rearrange to form new substances.
1.11	A substance that is used up	A reactant is a substance that is used up in a chemical reaction to form products.
1.12	Acidity or basicity	pH measures the acidity or basicity of a substance.
1.13	A neutral substance	Neutralization of an acid and a base produces a neutral substance, typically a salt and water.
1.14	Chemical change	Rusting is an example of a chemical change, where new substances are formed.
1.15	Change in color	A change in color is often a sign that a chemical reaction has taken place.
1.16	Endothermic reaction	An endothermic reaction absorbs energy, usually in the form of heat.
1.17	A substance burns in oxygen	Combustion is a chemical reaction where a substance burns in the presence of oxygen.
1.18	A mixture where substances are spread out evenly	A solution in chemistry is a mixture where substances are evenly distributed throughout.

1.19	Condensation	When a gas turns into a liquid, the process is called condensation.
1.20	Products	The new substances formed in a chemical reaction are called products.
1.21	One element replaces another	In a displacement reaction, one element replaces another in a compound.
1.22	Potential energy	The energy stored in chemical bonds is known as potential energy.
1.23	Transition point	The point in a reaction where reactants are turned into products is the transition point.
1.24	A solid that forms	A precipitate in a chemical reaction is a solid that forms and settles out of a liquid mixture.
1.25	A substance that changes color in different pH	An indicator in chemistry changes color in different pH environments to indicate acidity or basicity.
1.26	Photosynthesis	Photosynthesis is the process where plants convert sunlight into energy.
1.27	Oxygen	Oxygen is essential for combustion reactions to occur.
1.28	Physical change	Mixing substances without forming new substances is a physical change.
1.29	Oxidation	Oxidation is a reaction where a substance combines with oxygen, releasing energy.
1.30	A substance gains oxygen	In an oxidation reaction, a substance typically gains oxygen.
1.31	Endothermic reaction	An endothermic reaction absorbs energy, usually in the form of heat.
1.32	Shape change	Shape change is not typically a sign of a chemical reaction.
1.33	Neutralization	Neutralization occurs when acids and bases react together.
1.34	Law of Conservation of Mass	The Law of Conservation of Mass states that mass is conserved in a chemical reaction.
1.35	Inhibitor	A substance that slows down a chemical reaction is called an inhibitor.
1.36	Chemical changes create new substances	Chemical changes are characterized by the creation of new substances.
1.37	Exothermic reaction	An exothermic reaction releases heat.
1.38	They are rearranged	In a chemical reaction, atoms are rearranged to form new substances.
1.39	A substance made of two or more elements chemically combined	A compound is a substance formed when two or more elements are chemically bonded together.
1.40	Element	Different types of atoms are known as elements.

Topic 2 - Forces

2.1) What is a force?

☐ A push or a pull

☐ A type of energy

☐ A measurement of weight

☐ A kind of motion

2.2) What force pulls objects toward the Earth?

☐ Magnetism

☐ Friction

☐ Gravity

☐ Air resistance

2.3) What is friction?

☐ A force that speeds things up

☐ A force that pushes objects apart

☐ A force that resists motion

☐ A force that attracts metal

2.4) How does a magnet exert force?

☐ Through gravity

☐ Through light

☐ Through magnetic fields

☐ Through electricity

2.5) What is the force that opposes the motion of objects through air?

□ Gravity

□ Magnetism

□ Air resistance

□ Friction

2.6) What kind of force is needed to change the direction of a moving object?

□ A balanced force

□ An unbalanced force

□ A magnetic force

□ A gravitational force

2.7) What is inertia?

□ A type of energy

□ A force that moves objects

□ The tendency of an object to resist changes in its motion

□ The force of gravity on an object

2.8) What happens when two forces act in the same direction?

□ They cancel each other out

□ Their effects add up

□ One becomes stronger

□ They create a vacuum

2.9) What type of simple machine is a seesaw?

☐ Lever

☐ Pulley

☐ Wheel and axle

☐ Inclined plane

2.10) What is the term for the force that moves objects in a circular path?

☐ Centripetal force

☐ Centrifugal force

☐ Gravitational force

☐ Magnetic force

2.11) What does the law of universal gravitation state?

☐ All objects fall at the same rate

☐ Gravity is stronger in space

☐ Every object in the universe attracts every other object

☐ Gravity only acts on heavy objects

2.12) What kind of force is weight?

☐ Magnetic force

☐ Frictional force

☐ Gravitational force

☐ Electrical force

2.13) What is the force that acts between two touching objects?

☐ Gravity

☐ Air resistance

☐ Contact force

☐ Magnetic force

2.14) What happens to the gravitational force between two objects if their mass increases?

☐ It decreases

☐ It remains the same

☐ It increases

☐ It fluctuates

2.15) What is the term for a force that causes an object to move in a circle?

☐ Gravitational force

☐ Magnetic force

☐ Centripetal force

☐ Frictional force

2.16) What type of force slows down motion between two surfaces that are sliding past each other?

☐ Gravity

☐ Magnetism

☐ Friction

☐ Air resistance

2.17) What is the name of the force that pulls objects toward each other?

☐ Magnetism

☐ Gravity

☐ Friction

☐ Electrical force

2.18) What happens when two forces act in opposite directions?

☐ Their strength increases

☐ They create a new force

☐ Their effects are added together

☐ They cancel each other out

2.19) What is a balanced force?

☐ A force that causes a change in motion

☐ A force that does not cause a change in motion

☐ The strongest force acting on an object

☐ A force that only acts in space

2.20) What is the effect of air resistance on a falling object?

□ It causes the object to fall faster

□ It does not affect the object

□ It slows down the object

□ It changes the object's direction

2.21) What is the force that opposes the motion of an object through a fluid like air or water?

□ Gravity

□ Friction

□ Buoyancy

□ Drag

2.22) What is Newton's first law of motion also known as?

□ Law of Forces

□ Law of Gravity

□ Law of Inertia

□ Law of Acceleration

2.23) What is the upward force exerted by a fluid on an object in it?

□ Gravity

□ Friction

□ Buoyancy

□ Tension

2.24) What happens when an unbalanced force acts on an object?

☐ It stays still

☐ It moves at constant speed

☐ It changes its motion

☐ It changes its color

2.25) Which force is used to make a magnet stick to a refrigerator?

☐ Gravity

☐ Friction

☐ Magnetic force

☐ Electrical force

2.26) What is the measure of how difficult it is to stop a moving object?

☐ Weight

☐ Friction

☐ Inertia

☐ Momentum

2.27) What force keeps planets in orbit around the sun?

☐ Magnetic force

☐ Gravitational force

☐ Electrical force

☐ Nuclear force

2.28) What type of simple machine is a ramp?

☐ Lever

☐ Pulley

☐ Wheel and axle

☐ Inclined plane

2.29) What is needed to change the speed or direction of an object?

☐ An unbalanced force

☐ A balanced force

☐ No force

☐ A magnetic force

2.30) What do we call the force that acts on objects to pull them toward the center of the Earth?

☐ Magnetic force

☐ Gravity

☐ Friction

☐ Centripetal force

2.31) What is Newton's third law of motion?

☐ For every action, there is an equal and opposite reaction

☐ Objects at rest stay at rest

☐ Force equals mass times acceleration

☐ Every object attracts every other object

2.32) What does it mean when forces are 'balanced'?

☐ They cause a change in motion

☐ They cancel each other out and do not cause a change in motion

☐ They are all gravitational forces

☐ They always cause an object to move

2.33) What is the force that acts in the opposite direction to motion?

☐ Gravity

☐ Magnetism

☐ Friction

☐ Buoyancy

2.34) What is Newton's second law of motion?

☐ Force equals mass times acceleration

☐ For every action, there is an equal and opposite reaction

☐ Objects at rest stay at rest

☐ Every object attracts every other object

2.35) Which of these is a non-contact force?

☐ Friction

☐ Tension

☐ Gravity

☐ Air resistance

2.36) What kind of force is exerted by a coiled spring?

□ Elastic force

□ Gravitational force

□ Magnetic force

□ Buoyant force

2.37) What is the unit of force in the International System of Units?

□ Newton

□ Pascal

□ Joule

□ Watt

2.38) What happens when you rub your hands together quickly?

□ They cool down

□ They create light

□ They produce sound

□ They produce heat due to friction

2.39) What is a 'net force'?

□ The strongest force acting on an object

□ The combination of all forces acting on an object

□ The force that remains after all others cancel out

□ The first force applied to an object

ALEXANDER-GRACE EDUCATION

2.40) What effect does increasing the mass of an object have on its gravitational force?

□ Decreases the force

□ Has no effect

□ Increases the force

□ Changes the direction of the force

Topic 2 - Answers

Question Number	Answer	Explanation
2.1	A push or a pull	A force is a push or a pull exerted on an object.
2.2	Gravity	Gravity is the force that pulls objects toward the Earth.
2.3	A force that resists motion	Friction is a force that opposes the motion of objects.
2.4	Through magnetic fields	Magnets exert force through magnetic fields.
2.5	Air resistance	Air resistance is the force that opposes the motion of objects through air.
2.6	An unbalanced force	An unbalanced force is required to change the direction of a moving object.
2.7	The tendency of an object to resist changes in its motion	Inertia is the property of an object to resist changes in its state of motion.
2.8	Their effects add up	When two forces act in the same direction, their effects add up.
2.9	Lever	A seesaw is an example of a lever, a type of simple machine.
2.10	Centripetal force	Centripetal force is the force that keeps objects moving in a circular path.
2.11	Every object in the universe attracts every other object	The law of universal gravitation states that every object in the universe attracts every other object.
2.12	Gravitational force	Weight is the gravitational force exerted on an object.
2.13	Contact force	Contact force acts between two touching objects.
2.14	It increases	The gravitational force between two objects increases if their mass increases.
2.15	Centripetal force	Centripetal force causes an object to move in a circle.
2.16	Friction	Friction is the force that slows down motion between two surfaces sliding past each other.
2.17	Gravity	Gravity is the force that pulls objects toward each other.
2.18	They cancel each other out	When two forces act in opposite directions, they cancel each other out.
2.19	A force that does not cause a change in motion	A balanced force does not cause a change in an object's motion.

2.20	It slows down the object	Air resistance slows down a falling object.
2.21	Drag	Drag is the force that opposes the motion of an object through a fluid like air or water.
2.22	Law of Inertia	Newton's first law of motion is also known as the Law of Inertia.
2.23	Buoyancy	Buoyancy is the upward force exerted by a fluid on an object in it.
2.24	It changes its motion	An unbalanced force acting on an object changes its motion.
2.25	Magnetic force	Magnetic force is used to make a magnet stick to a refrigerator.
2.26	Inertia	Inertia measures how difficult it is to stop a moving object.
2.27	Gravitational force	Gravitational force keeps planets in orbit around the sun.
2.28	Inclined plane	A ramp is an example of an inclined plane, a type of simple machine.
2.29	An unbalanced force	An unbalanced force is needed to change the speed or direction of an object.
2.30	Gravity	Gravity is the force that pulls objects toward the center of the Earth.
2.31	For every action, there is an equal and opposite reaction	Newton's third law of motion states that for every action, there is an equal and opposite reaction.
2.32	They cancel each other out and do not cause a change in motion	When forces are balanced, they cancel each other out and do not cause a change in motion.
2.33	Friction	Friction is the force that acts in the opposite direction to motion.
2.34	Force equals mass times acceleration	Newton's second law of motion states that force equals mass times acceleration.
2.35	Gravity	Gravity is a non-contact force that acts between objects without them touching.
2.36	Elastic force	A coiled spring exerts an elastic force.
2.37	Newton	The unit of force in the International System of Units is the Newton.
2.38	They produce heat due to friction	Rubbing hands together quickly produces heat due to friction.
2.39	The combination of all forces acting on an object	The net force is the combination of all forces acting on an object.
2.40	Increases the force	Increasing the mass of an object increases its gravitational force.

Topic 3 – Electric Charges and Circuits

3.1) What is electricity?

☐ A type of energy

☐ A kind of magnet

☐ A form of light

☐ A type of gas

3.2) What are the two types of electric charges?

☐ Positive and negative

☐ North and south

☐ Hot and cold

☐ Fast and slow

3.3) What is a circuit?

☐ A type of battery

☐ A path through which electricity flows

☐ A kind of light bulb

☐ A switch

3.4) What happens in a 'closed' circuit?

☐ Electricity cannot flow

☐ Electricity flows freely

☐ The circuit overheats

☐ It turns into a magnet

ALEXANDER-GRACE EDUCATION

3.5) What is a conductor?

☐ A material that does not allow electricity to pass through

☐ A material that allows electricity to pass through

☐ A type of battery

☐ A type of switch

3.6) What is an insulator?

☐ A material that allows electricity to pass through

☐ A material that does not allow electricity to pass through

☐ A type of light bulb

☐ A type of wire

3.7) What is the purpose of a switch in a circuit?

☐ To increase the current

☐ To decrease the current

☐ To open or close the circuit

☐ To change the direction of the current

3.8) What creates a 'short circuit'?

☐ A break in the circuit

☐ Too many batteries

☐ A circuit that is too long

☐ An unintended path that allows electricity to flow where it shouldn't

3.9) What is static electricity?

☐ The flow of electric charge through a wire

☐ A buildup of electric charge on a surface

☐ Electricity created by magnets

☐ Electricity used in homes

3.10) How does a battery power a circuit?

☐ By heating the wires

☐ By providing a continuous flow of electric charge

☐ By creating a magnetic field

☐ By increasing the light in the circuit

3.11) What is the unit of electric current?

☐ Volt

☐ Watt

☐ Ampere

☐ Ohm

3.12) What happens when you rub a balloon on your hair?

☐ It creates sound

☐ It becomes heavier

☐ It creates static electricity

☐ It loses its color

3.13) What is the role of a resistor in a circuit?

□ To stop the electricity

□ To store electricity

□ To increase the flow of electricity

□ To reduce the flow of electricity

3.14) What is the difference between alternating current (AC) and direct current (DC)?

□ AC changes direction, DC does not

□ DC is safer than AC

□ AC is only used in cars

□ DC can't power electronics

3.15) What do you call a material that lets electricity flow through it easily?

□ Insulator

□ Conductor

□ Resistor

□ Capacitor

3.16) What is a parallel circuit?

□ A circuit with a single path for electricity

□ A circuit with multiple paths for electricity

□ A circuit with no paths for electricity

□ A circuit that only works at night

ALEXANDER-GRACE EDUCATION

3.17) What is the purpose of a fuse in a circuit?

☐ To increase electricity flow

☐ To prevent overloading of the circuit

☐ To make the circuit longer

☐ To connect two circuits

3.18) What causes a bulb in a circuit to light up?

☐ The presence of a battery

☐ The bulb getting hot

☐ Electric current flowing through it

☐ Static electricity

3.19) What is the effect of adding more bulbs in a series circuit?

☐ Increases the current

☐ Decreases the brightness of each bulb

☐ Has no effect on the brightness

☐ Makes the circuit a parallel circuit

3.20) What happens to the current in a series circuit if one component is removed or breaks?

☐ Current increases

☐ Current stops flowing

☐ Circuit becomes a parallel circuit

☐ Nothing changes

3.21) What material is commonly used to make wires in a circuit?

☐ Plastic

☐ Wood

☐ Copper

☐ Glass

3.22) What is the purpose of a voltmeter in a circuit?

☐ To measure the speed of electricity

☐ To measure the pressure of electricity

☐ To measure the resistance in the circuit

☐ To measure the electrical potential difference

3.23) How do electrons typically move in a circuit?

☐ From positive to negative

☐ From negative to positive

☐ In a random direction

☐ They do not move

3.24) What does a capacitor do in a circuit?

☐ Stores electrical energy temporarily

☐ Increases the voltage

☐ Converts AC to DC

☐ Connects two circuits together

3.25) What is the main difference between a series and parallel circuit?

☐ The number of batteries used

☐ The way components are arranged

☐ The type of electricity used

☐ The color of the wires

3.26) Why are insulators important in electrical devices?

☐ To make the device look better

☐ To prevent electrical shocks

☐ To increase the flow of electricity

☐ To make the device heavier

3.27) What happens to the resistance in a circuit if you add more resistors in series?

☐ Resistance decreases

☐ Resistance stays the same

☐ Resistance increases

☐ Resistance becomes zero

3.28) What is the role of a diode in a circuit?

☐ To allow current to flow in one direction

☐ To increase the current

☐ To store electricity

☐ To light up

3.29) What unit is used to measure electrical resistance?

☐ Volt

☐ Ampere

☐ Watt

☐ Ohm

3.30) What is an example of a good electrical insulator?

☐ Copper

☐ Water

☐ Rubber

☐ Iron

3.31) What is the main danger of a damaged electrical wire?

☐ It can become a tripping hazard

☐ It can cause an electrical fire

☐ It can become a magnet

☐ It can increase electricity costs

3.32) Why should water and electricity be kept apart?

☐ Water can make electricity stronger

☐ Water can stop the flow of electricity

☐ Water can conduct electricity and cause a shock

☐ Water can turn into steam

3.33) What is the main purpose of an electrical fuse?

☐ To make devices work faster

☐ To increase the current

☐ To protect circuits from too much current

☐ To store extra electricity

3.34) What is a common material used to insulate wires?

☐ Metal

☐ Glass

☐ Rubber

☐ Wood

3.35) What does LED stand for in light bulbs?

☐ Light Emitting Diode

☐ Low Energy Device

☐ Light Energy Design

☐ Long-Lasting Energy Device

3.36) How can you save energy at home?

☐ Use more electrical devices

☐ Leave lights on

☐ Unplug devices not in use

☐ Increase the brightness of screens

3.37) Why are batteries important in a circuit?

☐ They make the circuit look better

☐ They increase the weight of the circuit

☐ They provide a source of electrical energy

☐ They make the circuit more colorful

3.38) What happens if you touch a live electrical wire?

☐ You will get a prize

☐ It changes color

☐ You may get an electrical shock

☐ It becomes colder

3.39) Can electricity travel through air?

☐ Yes, in all conditions

☐ No, never

☐ Yes, but only under certain conditions

☐ Only in space

3.40) What should you do if you see a frayed electrical cord?

☐ Ignore it

☐ Touch it to check if it's live

☐ Report it to an adult or unplug it if safe

☐ Pour water on it to prevent a fire

Topic 3 - Answers

Question Number	Answer	Explanation
3.1	A type of energy	Electricity is a form of energy resulting from the existence of charged particles.
3.2	Positive and negative	Electric charges come in two types: positive and negative.
3.3	A path through which electricity flows	A circuit is a pathway that allows electricity to flow.
3.4	Electricity flows freely	In a closed circuit, electricity can flow unimpeded.
3.5	A material that allows electricity to pass through	Conductors are materials that permit the flow of electrical current.
3.6	A material that does not allow electricity to pass through	Insulators prevent the flow of electrical current.
3.7	To open or close the circuit	A switch is used to either allow or stop the flow of electricity in a circuit.
3.8	An unintended path that allows electricity to flow where it shouldn't	A short circuit occurs when electricity flows along an unintended path.
3.9	A buildup of electric charge on a surface	Static electricity is the result of an imbalance between negative and positive charges in an object.
3.10	By providing a continuous flow of electric charge	A battery powers a circuit by providing a steady flow of electrons.
3.11	Ampere	The unit of electric current is the ampere (A).
3.12	It creates static electricity	Rubbing a balloon on your hair causes a buildup of static electricity.
3.13	To reduce the flow of electricity	A resistor is used to decrease the current flowing through a circuit.
3.14	AC changes direction, DC does not	Alternating current (AC) changes direction periodically, while direct current (DC) flows in one direction.
3.15	Conductor	Conductors are materials that allow electricity to flow through them easily.
3.16	A circuit with multiple paths for electricity	In a parallel circuit, electricity has more than one path to travel.
3.17	To prevent overloading of the circuit	A fuse is designed to prevent excessive current flow, protecting the circuit.
3.18	Electric current flowing through it	A bulb lights up when electric current passes through it.

3.19	Decreases the brightness of each bulb	Adding more bulbs in a series circuit reduces the brightness of each bulb.
3.20	Current stops flowing	If a component in a series circuit is removed or breaks, the current stops flowing.
3.21	Copper	Copper is commonly used for making wires in circuits due to its excellent conductivity.
3.22	To measure the electrical potential difference	A voltmeter measures the difference in electrical potential between two points in a circuit.
3.23	From negative to positive	In a circuit, electrons typically flow from the negative to the positive terminal.
3.24	Stores electrical energy temporarily	A capacitor in a circuit temporarily stores electrical energy.
3.25	The way components are arranged	The main difference between series and parallel circuits is the arrangement of components.
3.26	To prevent electrical shocks	Insulators are important in electrical devices to prevent the risk of electrical shocks.
3.27	Resistance increases	Adding more resistors in series increases the overall resistance of the circuit.
3.28	To allow current to flow in one direction	A diode allows current to flow only in one direction in a circuit.
3.29	Ohm	The unit used to measure electrical resistance is the ohm (Ω).
3.30	Rubber	Rubber is an example of a good electrical insulator.
3.31	It can cause an electrical fire	A damaged electrical wire poses a risk of causing an electrical fire.
3.32	Water can conduct electricity and cause a shock	Water and electricity should be kept apart because water can conduct electricity, leading to electric shocks.
3.33	To protect circuits from too much current	An electrical fuse is used to protect a circuit from excessive current flow.
3.34	Rubber	Rubber is commonly used to insulate wires due to its insulating properties.
3.35	Light Emitting Diode	LED stands for Light Emitting Diode and is used in energy-efficient light bulbs.
3.36	Unplug devices not in use	Unplugging devices not in use is an effective way to save energy at home.
3.37	They provide a source of electrical energy	Batteries are important in a circuit as they supply the electrical energy needed to power the circuit.
3.38	You may get an electrical shock	Touching a live electrical wire can result in an electrical shock.
3.39	Yes, but only under certain conditions	Electricity can travel through air under specific conditions, such as high voltage or when a spark is created.
3.40	Report it to an adult or unplug it if safe	If you see a frayed electrical cord, it should be reported to an adult or unplugged if it is safe to do so.

ALEXANDER-GRACE EDUCATION

Topic 4 – Energy Forms

4.1) What is energy?

☐ The ability to do work

☐ A type of machine

☐ A measurement of speed

☐ A kind of liquid

4.2) What is kinetic energy?

☐ Energy of motion

☐ Energy stored in objects

☐ Energy from the sun

☐ Energy from food

4.3) What is potential energy?

☐ Energy of motion

☐ Energy stored in objects

☐ Energy from heat

☐ Energy from light

4.4) What is thermal energy?

☐ Energy of movement in particles of matter

☐ Energy from the sun

☐ Energy from water

☐ Energy from wind

4.5) How is sound energy produced?

☐ By eating food

☐ By moving objects

☐ By vibrations

☐ By sunlight

4.6) What is electrical energy?

☐ Energy from batteries

☐ Energy from moving air

☐ Energy from water

☐ Energy from food

4.7) What is light energy?

☐ Energy that we can see

☐ Energy from sleeping

☐ Energy from food

☐ Energy from water

4.8) How does solar energy reach the Earth?

☐ Through water

☐ As light and heat from the sun

☐ Through sound

☐ Through cables

4.9) What can we use to measure energy?

□ A ruler

□ A scale

□ A thermometer

□ A joulemeter

4.10) What form of energy is in food?

□ Kinetic energy

□ Thermal energy

□ Chemical energy

□ Sound energy

4.11) What is renewable energy?

□ Energy that can be reused

□ Energy that can't be reused

□ Energy from non-natural sources

□ Energy from artificial lights

4.12) Give an example of a renewable energy source.

□ Coal

□ Natural gas

□ Solar power

□ Batteries

4.13) What is non-renewable energy?

□ Energy that can be reused

□ Energy that cannot be easily replenished

□ Energy from the sun

□ Energy from wind

4.14) Give an example of a non-renewable energy source.

□ Solar power

□ Wind power

□ Coal

□ Hydroelectric power

4.15) What is the main difference between renewable and non-renewable energy?

□ Renewable energy is always safe

□ Non-renewable energy is cheaper

□ Renewable energy can be replenished naturally

□ Non-renewable energy is always clean

4.16) What is mechanical energy?

□ Energy from machines

□ Energy from movement and position

□ Energy from heat

□ Energy from light

4.17) How is wind energy harnessed?

☐ Through solar panels

☐ Through water wheels

☐ Through wind turbines

☐ Through batteries

4.18) What is the main use of hydroelectric energy?

☐ To produce sound

☐ To heat water

☐ To generate electricity

☐ To cool buildings

4.19) How does a plant get energy?

☐ From the soil

☐ From water

☐ From the air

☐ From sunlight through photosynthesis

4.20) What type of energy is used by a car engine?

☐ Solar energy

☐ Wind energy

☐ Chemical energy from fuel

☐ Hydroelectric energy

4.21) What is the main difference between renewable and non-renewable energy?

□ Renewable energy is cheaper

□ Non-renewable energy is always from the sun

□ Renewable energy can be replenished

□ Non-renewable energy is safer

4.22) What is the primary source of geothermal energy?

□ The sun

□ The Earth's core

□ The wind

□ Water

4.23) What is biomass energy?

□ Energy from living or recently living organisms

□ Energy from the sun

□ Energy from wind

□ Energy from water

4.24) How does a hydroelectric power plant generate electricity?

□ Using solar panels

□ By burning coal

□ Using the energy of moving water

□ Through nuclear reactions

4.25) What type of energy is stored in fossil fuels?

□ Kinetic energy

□ Solar energy

□ Chemical energy

□ Thermal energy

4.26) Why is conserving energy important?

□ To make energy more expensive

□ To protect the environment and save resources

□ To make devices run faster

□ To increase pollution

4.27) What is an example of using solar energy?

□ Driving a car

□ Using a microwave

□ Cooking food in a solar oven

□ Watching television

4.28) Can energy be converted from one form to another?

□ No, it's impossible

□ Yes, but only in space

□ Yes, energy can be converted

□ No, it's illegal

4.29) What form of energy does a fan convert electrical energy into?

☐ Light energy

☐ Chemical energy

☐ Kinetic energy

☐ Thermal energy

4.30) How is energy from the wind used?

☐ To create waves in the ocean

☐ To move cars

☐ To generate electricity

☐ To produce food

4.31) What is the role of a turbine in generating electricity?

☐ To store energy

☐ To heat water

☐ To convert kinetic energy into electrical energy

☐ To cool down the generator

4.32) What kind of energy do plants use to make their own food?

☐ Kinetic energy

☐ Thermal energy

☐ Chemical energy

☐ Solar energy

4.33) Why are solar panels important?

□ They make houses look better

□ They reduce the need for electricity

□ They convert solar energy into electricity

□ They are used for cooking

4.34) What is a disadvantage of using fossil fuels?

□ They are very cheap

□ They last forever

□ They contribute to pollution

□ They are very colorful

4.35) How do wind turbines generate electricity?

□ By burning fuel

□ By using solar energy

□ By converting wind energy into electrical energy

□ By using water

4.36) What is a natural resource?

□ A man-made energy source

□ A resource that comes from nature

□ A type of food

□ A kind of medicine

4.37) What does 'sustainable energy' mean?

☐ Energy that is dangerous

☐ Energy that lasts for a short time

☐ Energy that can be sustained without harming the environment

☐ Expensive energy

4.38) What type of energy is released when fuel is burned?

☐ Solar energy

☐ Kinetic energy

☐ Chemical energy

☐ Mechanical energy

4.39) How does a refrigerator use energy?

☐ It converts chemical energy into light

☐ It uses kinetic energy to cook food

☐ It uses electrical energy to produce cold

☐ It uses solar energy to make ice

4.40) What is the main function of batteries in electronic devices?

☐ To make them heavier

☐ To allow them to operate without a direct power source

☐ To make them look modern

☐ To increase their size

Topic 4 - Answers

Question Number	Answer	Explanation
4.1	The ability to do work	Energy is defined as the capacity to do work or produce change.
4.2	Energy of motion	Kinetic energy is the energy an object possesses due to its motion.
4.3	Energy stored in objects	Potential energy is the energy stored in an object due to its position or state.
4.4	Energy of movement in particles of matter	Thermal energy is the energy that comes from the movement of atoms and molecules in matter.
4.5	By vibrations	Sound energy is produced through vibrations in a medium such as air, water, or solids.
4.6	Energy from batteries	Electrical energy is the energy derived from electric potential energy or kinetic energy of charged particles.
4.7	Energy that we can see	Light energy is the form of energy that is visible to the human eye.
4.8	As light and heat from the sun	Solar energy reaches the Earth as light and heat from the sun.
4.9	A joulemeter	Energy can be measured with a device known as a joulemeter.
4.10	Chemical energy	The energy in food is stored as chemical energy, which organisms use for their activities.
4.11	Energy that can be reused	Renewable energy refers to energy sources that can be replenished or renewed naturally over time.
4.12	Solar power	Solar power is an example of a renewable energy source, as it is replenished by the sun.
4.13	Energy that cannot be easily replenished	Non-renewable energy refers to sources that do not replenish quickly or are finite.
4.14	Coal	Coal is an example of a non-renewable energy source, as it is not replenished rapidly.
4.15	Renewable energy can be replenished naturally	The main difference is that renewable energy sources can be naturally replenished.
4.16	Energy from movement and position	Mechanical energy is the energy due to the movement and position of an object.
4.17	Through wind turbines	Wind energy is harnessed using wind turbines that convert the wind's kinetic energy into electricity.
4.18	To generate electricity	Hydroelectric energy is primarily used to generate electricity using water flow.

4.19	From sunlight through photosynthesis	Plants get their energy from sunlight through the process of photosynthesis.
4.20	Chemical energy from fuel	A car engine uses the chemical energy stored in fuel to operate.
4.21	Renewable energy can be replenished	Renewable energy sources can be naturally replenished, unlike non-renewable sources.
4.22	The Earth's core	Geothermal energy is derived from the heat inside the Earth's core.
4.23	Energy from living or recently living organisms	Biomass energy is derived from organic materials like plants and animal waste.
4.24	Using the energy of moving water	Hydroelectric power plants generate electricity by harnessing the energy of moving water.
4.25	Chemical energy	Fossil fuels store chemical energy formed from ancient organic matter.
4.26	To protect the environment and save resources	Conserving energy is crucial for protecting the environment and preserving natural resources.
4.27	Cooking food in a solar oven	Using a solar oven to cook food is an example of utilizing solar energy.
4.28	Yes, energy can be converted	Energy can be converted from one form to another, like electrical to mechanical energy.
4.29	Kinetic energy	A fan converts electrical energy into kinetic energy (motion).
4.30	To generate electricity	Wind energy is primarily used for generating electricity.
4.31	To convert kinetic energy into electrical energy	Turbines convert the kinetic energy of water, steam, or wind into electrical energy.
4.32	Solar energy	Plants use solar energy in photosynthesis to make their own food.
4.33	They convert solar energy into electricity	Solar panels are important as they convert solar energy into usable electricity.
4.34	They contribute to pollution	A disadvantage of using fossil fuels is their contribution to environmental pollution.
4.35	By converting wind energy into electrical energy	Wind turbines generate electricity by converting the kinetic energy of wind.
4.36	A resource that comes from nature	Natural resources are materials provided by Earth that can be used to produce energy or goods.
4.37	Energy that can be sustained without harming the environment	Sustainable energy refers to energy sources that don't harm the environment and can be used over the long term.
4.38	Chemical energy	When fuel is burned, it releases stored chemical energy.
4.39	It uses electrical energy to produce cold	A refrigerator uses electrical energy to maintain a cold environment inside.
4.40	To allow them to operate without a direct power source	Batteries enable electronic devices to operate without being connected to a direct power source.

Topic 5 – Magnetism and Electromagnetism

5.1) What is a magnet?

☐ A type of battery

☐ A material that attracts iron and some other materials

☐ A kind of light

☐ A type of electricity

5.2) What are the two ends of a magnet called?

☐ East and West

☐ North and South poles

☐ Top and Bottom

☐ Left and Right

5.3) What materials are attracted to magnets?

☐ Plastic and wood

☐ Glass and paper

☐ Iron, nickel, and cobalt

☐ Rubber and clay

5.4) What is an electromagnet?

☐ A natural magnet

☐ A type of battery

☐ A magnet made by electric current

☐ A magnet that works only in sunlight

5.5) How can you make a simple electromagnet?

☐ By rubbing a magnet on a nail

☐ By putting a nail near a battery

☐ By wrapping a wire around a nail and connecting it to a battery

☐ By heating a piece of iron

5.6) What happens if you break a magnet in half?

☐ It stops being a magnet

☐ It becomes an electromagnet

☐ Each half becomes a smaller magnet with its own north and south poles

☐ It loses its color

5.7) Can the Earth be considered a giant magnet?

☐ No, because it's too big

☐ Yes, it has a magnetic field

☐ Only when it's daytime

☐ Only in winter

5.8) Why do compass needles point north?

☐ Because of gravity

☐ Because of the wind

☐ Because they align with the Earth's magnetic field

☐ Because they are painted that way

5.9) What is a magnetic field?

☐ The area around a magnet where its force can be felt

☐ A field where magnets grow

☐ The space inside a magnet

☐ A playground for magnets

5.10) Can magnets attract all metal objects?

☐ Yes, all metals

☐ Only gold and silver

☐ No, only some like iron, nickel, and cobalt

☐ Only when heated

5.11) What is a temporary magnet?

☐ A magnet that lasts forever

☐ A magnet that only works in the dark

☐ A magnet made from a material that quickly loses its magnetism

☐ A natural magnet

5.12) What is a permanent magnet?

☐ A magnet that cannot be turned off

☐ A magnet that only works in the light

☐ A magnet that loses its magnetism easily

☐ A magnet made from paper

5.13) What are magnetic poles?

☐ The strongest parts of a magnet

☐ The middle of a magnet

☐ The ends of a magnetic field

☐ The corners of a magnet

5.14) What happens when opposite poles of two magnets are brought close together?

☐ They repel each other

☐ They create electricity

☐ They attract each other

☐ They become hotter

5.15) What is the effect of heating a magnet?

☐ It becomes stronger

☐ It can lose its magnetic properties

☐ It turns into an electromagnet

☐ It changes color

5.16) Can magnets attract objects through other materials?

☐ No, they need direct contact

☐ Yes, through materials like paper or plastic

☐ Only through metal

☐ Only through water

5.17) Why does a compass point north?

☐ It is programmed to do so

☐ Because of the sun's position

☐ Due to the Earth's magnetic field aligning the needle

☐ Because of the moon's gravity

5.18) Can magnets work in space?

☐ No, they need air

☐ Yes, magnets work in space

☐ Only on planets

☐ Only in water

5.19) What is a magnetic force?

☐ The force a magnet uses to pull objects

☐ The force to push a magnet

☐ The force to break a magnet

☐ The force to heat a magnet

5.20) What is the area around a magnet where magnetic forces can be felt called?

☐ Magnetic zone

☐ Magnetic field

☐ Magnetic land

☐ Magnetic area

5.21) What happens when you put the north pole of one magnet close to the north pole of another magnet?

□ They attract each other

□ They create light

□ They repel each other

□ They become one big magnet

5.22) What is a compass primarily used for?

□ Measuring temperature

□ Finding direction

□ Measuring distance

□ Looking at stars

5.23) What is a magnetic material?

□ A material that cannot be magnetized

□ A material that is naturally a magnet

□ A material that can be attracted to a magnet

□ A material that repels magnets

5.24) Can a magnet attract all types of metal?

□ Yes, all metals

□ No, only magnetic metals like iron, nickel, and cobalt

□ Only gold and silver

□ Only in water

5.25) What are bar magnets typically used for?

☐ Cooking

☐ Educational purposes and experiments

☐ Holding papers on a fridge

☐ Lighting up rooms

5.26) How can you weaken a magnet?

☐ By painting it

☐ By dropping it or heating it

☐ By using it too much

☐ By putting it in water

5.27) What does it mean when we say magnets have polarity?

☐ They have a positive and negative side

☐ They have north and south poles

☐ They can only attract

☐ They are very strong

5.28) How is Earth's magnetic field useful to us?

☐ It keeps the planet warm

☐ It helps in navigation and protects us from solar wind

☐ It makes the Earth spin

☐ It attracts the moon

5.29) What is one way to make a magnet?

☐ Freezing a piece of metal

☐ Heating a piece of metal

☐ Stroking a piece of iron with a magnet

☐ Burying metal underground

5.30) Why do magnets stick to a refrigerator?

☐ Because of the paint on the fridge

☐ Because the fridge is cold

☐ Because the fridge is made of a magnetic material

☐ Because of electricity

5.31) What is a natural magnet?

☐ A magnet made in factories

☐ A magnet found in nature, like lodestone

☐ Any type of metal

☐ A magnet made of plastic

5.32) How can you demagnetize a magnet?

☐ By painting it

☐ By freezing it

☐ By heating it or striking it

☐ By keeping it in the dark

5.33) Why do magnets stick to some refrigerators?

☐ Because of the light inside the fridge

☐ Because of the electricity in the fridge

☐ Because the refrigerator is usually made of a magnetic material

☐ Because of the color of the fridge

5.34) Can magnets affect electrical devices?

☐ No, they have no effect

☐ Yes, they can interfere with or damage some devices

☐ Only if the device is turned off

☐ Only in water

5.35) What is the invisible area around a magnet where its force affects other objects called?

☐ Magnetic zone

☐ Magnetic field

☐ Magnetic sphere

☐ Magnetic ring

5.36) Are all metals magnetic?

☐ Yes, all metals

☐ No, only some like iron, nickel, and cobalt

☐ Only gold and silver

☐ Only metals that are red

5.37) What is a horseshoe magnet?

□ A magnet in the shape of a horse

□ A magnet that can only attract horseshoes

□ A magnet shaped like a 'U'

□ A magnet used only by cowboys

5.38) How does a magnetic levitation train (maglev) work?

□ By using wings

□ By using hot air

□ Using magnetic fields to lift and move the train

□ By using lots of wheels

5.39) Can magnets lose their magnetism over time?

□ No, they last forever

□ Yes, especially if they are heated or hit

□ Only if they are blue

□ Only if they are used every day

5.40) What is the effect of placing a piece of paper between a magnet and a magnetic object?

□ The magnet becomes stronger

□ The paper turns into a magnet

□ The magnet can still attract the object through the paper

□ The object becomes demagnetized

Topic 5 - Answers

Question Number	Answer	Explanation
5.1	A material that attracts iron and some other materials	A magnet is defined by its ability to attract certain metals like iron.
5.2	North and South poles	The two ends of a magnet are referred to as the North and South poles.
5.3	Iron, nickel, and cobalt	Magnets are known to attract materials such as iron, nickel, and cobalt.
5.4	A magnet made by electric current	An electromagnet is created by passing an electric current through a coil of wire.
5.5	By wrapping a wire around a nail and connecting it to a battery	This is a simple way to create an electromagnet.
5.6	Each half becomes a smaller magnet with its own north and south poles	Breaking a magnet results in two smaller magnets, each with its own poles.
5.7	Yes, it has a magnetic field	The Earth acts like a giant magnet, having its own magnetic field.
5.8	Because they align with the Earth's magnetic field	Compass needles point north due to the alignment with Earth's magnetic field.
5.9	The area around a magnet where its force can be felt	A magnetic field is the area surrounding a magnet where magnetic forces are exerted.
5.10	No, only some like iron, nickel, and cobalt	Magnets do not attract all metals but only specific types like iron, nickel, and cobalt.
5.11	A magnet made from a material that quickly loses its magnetism	Temporary magnets are those that do not retain their magnetic properties for long.
5.12	A magnet that cannot be turned off	Permanent magnets maintain their magnetism over time without external influence.
5.13	The ends of a magnetic field	Magnetic poles are the points at the ends of a magnet where the magnetic force is strongest.
5.14	They attract each other	Opposite poles of magnets attract each other.
5.15	It can lose its magnetic properties	Heating a magnet can cause it to lose its magnetism.
5.16	Yes, through materials like paper or plastic	Magnets can attract magnetic objects through various materials, including paper and plastic.
5.17	Due to the Earth's magnetic field aligning the needle	A compass points north because its needle aligns with the Earth's magnetic field.
5.18	Yes, magnets work in space	Magnets function in space as magnetic forces are not dependent on the Earth's atmosphere.

5.19	The force a magnet uses to pull objects	Magnetic force is the force exerted by a magnet to attract or repel other magnetic materials.
5.20	Magnetic field	The magnetic field is the area around a magnet where its magnetic forces can be detected.
5.21	They repel each other	Like poles of magnets repel each other.
5.22	Finding direction	A compass is primarily used for navigation, to find direction.
5.23	A material that can be attracted to a magnet	Magnetic materials are those that can be influenced or attracted by a magnet.
5.24	No, only magnetic metals like iron, nickel, and cobalt	Magnets do not attract all types of metals, only specific magnetic ones.
5.25	Educational purposes and experiments	Bar magnets are commonly used for demonstration and educational purposes in magnetic experiments.
5.26	By dropping it or heating it	Magnets can be weakened by physical impact (like dropping) or by heating.
5.27	They have north and south poles	Polarity in magnets refers to the presence of north and south poles.
5.28	It helps in navigation and protects us from solar wind	Earth's magnetic field is crucial for navigation and protects the planet from solar winds.
5.29	Stroking a piece of iron with a magnet	This method can magnetize a piece of iron, turning it into a magnet.
5.30	Because the fridge is made of a magnetic material	Magnets stick to refrigerators because they are made of materials that magnets can attract.
5.31	A magnet found in nature, like lodestone	Natural magnets, like lodestone, are found in nature and exhibit magnetic properties.
5.32	By heating it or striking it	Heating or striking a magnet can demagnetize it.
5.33	Because the refrigerator is usually made of a magnetic material	Magnets stick to refrigerators due to the magnetic nature of the materials used in refrigerators.
5.34	Yes, they can interfere with or damage some devices	Magnets can affect the functioning of some electrical devices.
5.35	Magnetic field	The magnetic field is the invisible area around a magnet where its force affects other objects.
5.36	No, only some like iron, nickel, and cobalt	Not all metals are magnetic; only specific ones like iron, nickel, and cobalt are attracted to magnets.
5.37	A magnet shaped like a 'U'	A horseshoe magnet is shaped like a 'U', and it is a type of permanent magnet.
5.38	Using magnetic fields to lift and move the train	Maglev trains use magnetic levitation for lifting and propulsion.
5.39	Yes, especially if they are heated or hit	Magnets can lose their magnetism over time, especially if mishandled.
5.40	The magnet can still attract the object through the paper	Magnets can attract magnetic objects through non-magnetic materials like paper.

Topic 6 – Motion

6.1) What is motion?

□ Staying in one place

□ The change in position of an object over time

□ Making noise

□ Changing color

6.2) What causes an object to start moving?

□ Always gravity

□ A push or a pull (force)

□ Being round

□ Being light

6.3) What is speed?

□ How heavy something is

□ How loud something is

□ How fast an object is moving

□ The color of an object

6.4) How do you calculate speed?

□ Distance divided by time

□ Time divided by distance

□ Weight times height

□ Age of the object

6.5) What is a force?

☐ A type of motion

☐ A type of food

☐ A push or pull that can cause an object to move, stop, or change direction

☐ A color

6.6) What is gravity?

☐ A type of force that pulls objects toward each other

☐ A type of light

☐ A type of magnet

☐ A type of plant

6.7) What happens when forces are balanced?

☐ The object moves faster

☐ The object changes color

☐ The object does not move or changes its motion

☐ The object gets heavier

6.8) What is friction?

☐ A force that speeds things up

☐ A force that occurs when two objects rub against each other

☐ The sound something makes

☐ The color of an object when it moves

6.9) How can you increase friction?

□ By making surfaces smoother

□ By painting the surfaces

□ By making surfaces rougher or using a material like rubber

□ By adding light

6.10) What is inertia?

□ The tendency of an object to resist changes in its motion

□ The speed of an object

□ The color of an object when it moves

□ The sound an object makes

6.11) What is an example of a moving object changing direction?

□ A ball rolling downhill

□ A car turning a corner

□ A book sitting on a table

□ A tree growing

6.12) What is momentum?

□ The color of a moving object

□ The sound made by a moving object

□ The force that stops movement

□ The quantity of motion an object has

6.13) What does 'acceleration' mean in terms of motion?

☐ Slowing down

☐ Changing direction or speed of an object

☐ Stopping completely

☐ Making no movement

6.14) Can an object be moving if it's not changing its position?

☐ Yes, always

☐ No, movement means changing position

☐ Only in space

☐ Only if it's very small

6.15) How does mass affect motion?

☐ It doesn't affect motion

☐ The greater the mass, the easier it is to move

☐ The greater the mass, the more force needed to move it

☐ Mass changes the color of motion

6.16) What is a simple machine?

☐ A very small machine

☐ A device that makes work easier by changing the direction or magnitude of a force

☐ A machine that uses electricity

☐ A toy

6.17) How do wheels help with motion?

☐ They make things heavier

☐ They change the color of objects

☐ They reduce friction and make it easier to move objects

☐ They make noise

6.18) What is the relationship between force and motion?

☐ Force can cause motion, stop motion, or change the direction of motion

☐ Force makes objects lighter

☐ There is no relationship

☐ Force changes the color of objects

6.19) What happens to the speed of an object if no forces act on it?

☐ It becomes zero

☐ It changes color

☐ It remains constant

☐ It increases automatically

6.20) What is a pulley?

☐ A type of food

☐ A machine that uses a wheel and a rope to help lift things

☐ A button on a machine

☐ A light on a vehicle

6.21) What is the difference between speed and velocity?

□ Speed is faster than velocity

□ Speed is the same as velocity

□ Speed is how fast something moves, velocity includes direction

□ Velocity is only for cars

6.22) What is a lever?

□ A simple machine that helps to lift heavy objects

□ A type of wheel

□ A button on a machine

□ A type of screw

6.23) How does a ramp make moving objects easier?

□ By changing their color

□ By making them lighter

□ By allowing to move objects over a gentler slope, reducing the force needed

□ By making them smaller

6.24) What is air resistance?

□ A type of smell in the air

□ The force of air pushing against a moving object

□ The sound air makes

□ The color of air

6.25) What is the purpose of gears in a machine?

☐ To make the machine look nicer

☐ To make noise

☐ To transfer motion and force from one part to another

☐ To hold pieces together

6.26) What happens when two objects collide?

☐ They change color

☐ They always break

☐ They exert forces on each other, often changing their motion

☐ They become lighter

6.27) What is a wedge?

☐ A simple machine that helps to split, lift, or hold objects

☐ A type of wheel

☐ A button on a computer

☐ A type of food

6.28) How does lubrication reduce friction?

☐ By making surfaces sticky

☐ By increasing the temperature

☐ By adding a substance to make surfaces smoother and reduce the force of friction

☐ By painting surfaces

6.29) What role does friction play in walking?

☐ It makes walking harder

☐ It changes the color of shoes

☐ It helps grip the ground, preventing slipping

☐ It makes shoes heavier

6.30) How does gravity affect motion on Earth?

☐ It makes things go sideways

☐ It pulls everything towards the center of the Earth

☐ It lights things up

☐ It makes sounds louder

6.31) What does 'centripetal force' mean?

☐ A force that pushes objects away from the center

☐ A force that pulls objects toward the center of a circle

☐ A force that stops motion

☐ A force that makes objects heavier

6.32) What is the role of wheels and axles in motion?

☐ To increase friction

☐ To make objects heavier

☐ To reduce friction and help things move more easily

☐ To change the color of motion

6.33) Can motion be in a straight line only?

☐ Yes, always

☐ No, motion can be in any direction, including circular

☐ Only on Tuesdays

☐ Only in water

6.34) What is Newton's first law of motion?

☐ Objects in motion stay in motion, objects at rest stay at rest unless acted upon by a force

☐ For every action, there is an equal and opposite reaction

☐ Force equals mass times acceleration

☐ Motion always causes friction

6.35) How does a screw help with motion?

☐ It makes things stick together

☐ It increases friction

☐ It converts a rotational force into a forward or backward motion

☐ It changes the color of objects

6.36) What is Newton's second law of motion?

☐ Objects in motion stay in motion

☐ For every action, there is an equal and opposite reaction

☐ Force equals mass times acceleration

☐ Gravity pulls everything down

6.37) How do seat belts help in a moving car?

☐ They make the car go faster

☐ They keep passengers in place, reducing the risk during sudden stops or changes in motion

☐ They change the direction of motion

☐ They play music

6.38) What is 'moment of force'?

☐ When a force is applied for a minute

☐ The feeling of force

☐ The turning effect produced by a force

☐ The sound of a force

6.39) What happens when you jump on a trampoline?

☐ You create light

☐ You go into space

☐ Your body converts potential energy to kinetic energy and back

☐ You become heavier

6.40) What is a fulcrum?

☐ A type of food

☐ The point on which a lever rests or is supported and on which it pivots

☐ A button on a machine

☐ A light on a vehicle

Topic 6 - Answers

Question Number	Answer	Explanation
6.1	The change in position of an object over time	Motion is when something moves or changes its place. It's not staying still, making noise, or changing color.
6.2	A push or a pull (force)	An object starts moving because of a force, like pushing or pulling it. Gravity is just one type of force.
6.3	How fast an object is moving	Speed tells us how quickly something is moving. It's not about its weight, loudness, or color.
6.4	Distance divided by time	To find out speed, we see how far something goes (distance) and how long it takes (time).
6.5	A push or pull that can cause an object to move, stop, or change direction	A force is something that can make things move, stop, or change how they're moving. It's not a type of food or color.
6.6	A type of force that pulls objects toward each other	Gravity is the force that makes things fall or stay on the ground. It's not light, a magnet, or a plant.
6.7	The object does not move or changes its motion	When forces are balanced, they cancel out, so the object won't start moving or change how it's moving.
6.8	A force that occurs when two objects rub against each other	Friction is what we feel when things rub together. It doesn't speed things up or make noise.
6.9	By making surfaces rougher or using a material like rubber	Making surfaces rougher increases friction, which helps prevent slipping.
6.10	The tendency of an object to resist changes in its motion	Inertia is why things keep doing what they're doing (like staying still or moving) until a force acts on them.
6.11	A car turning a corner	When a car turns, it's changing direction. A rolling ball or a growing tree isn't changing direction.
6.12	The quantity of motion an object has	Momentum is about how much movement an object has. It's not about sound, color, or stopping movement.
6.13	Changing direction or speed of an object	Acceleration means speeding up, slowing down, or turning. It's not about stopping or staying still.
6.14	No, movement means changing position	If something isn't changing its place, it's not moving. It's the same everywhere, even in space or if it's small.
6.15	The greater the mass, the more force needed to move it	Heavier things (greater mass) need more force to move. Mass doesn't change how things look.
6.16	A device that makes work easier by changing the direction or magnitude of a force	Simple machines like levers or pulleys make it easier to do work. They're not just small or electric machines.
6.17	They reduce friction and make it easier to move objects	Wheels help move things more easily by cutting down on friction. They don't change color or make noise.

6.18	Force can cause motion, stop motion, or change the direction of motion	Forces affect how things move, whether they start, stop, or turn. They don't change objects' weight or color.
6.19	It remains constant	If no forces are acting, an object keeps moving at the same speed. It doesn't stop or change color.
6.20	A machine that uses a wheel and a rope to help lift things	A pulley uses a wheel and a rope to make lifting things easier. It's not food, a button, or a light.
6.21	Speed is how fast something moves, velocity includes direction	Speed is just how fast, but velocity also tells us which way something is going. It's not only for cars.
6.22	A simple machine that helps to lift heavy objects	A lever makes it easier to lift things. It's not a wheel, button, or screw.
6.23	By allowing to move objects over a gentler slope, reducing the force needed	Ramps make it easier to move things up by spreading the effort over a longer distance.
6.24	The force of air pushing against a moving object	Air resistance is the air pushing against something that's moving. It's not a smell, sound, or color.
6.25	To transfer motion and force from one part to another	Gears in machines move force and motion around. They're not just for looks or noise.
6.26	They exert forces on each other, often changing their motion	When objects collide, they push on each other and can change how they're moving.
6.27	A simple machine that helps to split, lift, or hold objects	A wedge can split things apart or hold them. It's not a wheel, button, or food.
6.28	By adding a substance to make surfaces smoother and reduce the force of friction	Lubrication makes surfaces slick so they rub together less. It doesn't make things sticky or hot.
6.29	It helps grip the ground, preventing slipping	Friction from the ground helps us walk without slipping. It doesn't make it harder or change shoe color.
6.30	It pulls everything towards the center of the Earth	Gravity pulls us and everything else towards the Earth's center. It doesn't affect light or sound.
6.31	A force that pulls objects toward the center of a circle	Centripetal force pulls things towards the center when they're moving in a circle.
6.32	To reduce friction and help things move more easily	Wheels and axles make it easier for things to roll, reducing friction.
6.33	No, motion can be in any direction, including circular	Things can move in any direction, not just straight. They can even go round and round.
6.34	Objects in motion stay in motion, objects at rest stay at rest unless acted upon by a force	Newton's first law tells us that things keep doing what they're doing unless a force changes that.
6.35	It converts a rotational force into a forward or backward motion	A screw turns a twist into a straight-line movement. It doesn't just stick things or change colors.
6.36	Force equals mass times acceleration	Newton's second law says that to move something heavier (more mass), you need more force.
6.37	They keep passengers in place, reducing the risk during sudden stops or changes in motion	Seat belts hold you in your seat in a car, especially when it stops quickly or turns.
6.38	The turning effect produced by a force	Moment of force is about how a force can make something spin or turn.

| 6.39 | Your body converts potential energy to kinetic energy and back | Jumping on a trampoline turns stored energy into movement energy and back again. |
| 6.40 | The point on which a lever rests or is supported and on which it pivots | The fulcrum is the point where a lever turns. It's not food, a button, or a light. |

Topic 7 – Pure Substances, Mixtures, and Solutions

7.1) What is a pure substance?

☐ A substance made of only one kind of material

☐ Any liquid

☐ Any solid material

☐ A mixture of different things

7.2) Can you separate a mixture easily?

☐ No, it's impossible

☐ Yes, because it's made of different substances that are not chemically combined

☐ Only with a machine

☐ Only if it's a liquid

7.3) What is a solution?

☐ A type of machine

☐ A solid mixed with a liquid

☐ A mixture where one substance dissolves in another

☐ A problem in science

7.4) What is an example of a pure substance?

☐ Salt water

☐ Air

☐ Gold

☐ Salad

7.5) How is a solution different from other mixtures?

☐ It can only be a liquid

☐ It is always clear

☐ The substances in a solution are evenly distributed and don't settle out

☐ It is only made of solids

7.6) What is a solvent in a solution?

☐ The part that gets dissolved

☐ The liquid in which the solute is dissolved

☐ The container that holds the solution

☐ A tool used to make solutions

7.7) What is a solute in a solution?

☐ The part that does the dissolving

☐ The container that holds the solution

☐ The substance that is dissolved in the solvent

☐ A type of solvent

7.8) What is a mixture?

☐ A pure substance

☐ A type of solution

☐ A combination of two or more substances that are not chemically combined

☐ A type of machine

7.9) What happens when salt is dissolved in water?

☐ The water freezes

☐ The salt and water become a solution

☐ The water turns into air

☐ The salt disappears forever

7.10) Can mixtures be separated into their original substances?

☐ No, they become a new substance

☐ Yes, because they are not chemically combined

☐ Only if they are heated

☐ Only if they are frozen

7.11) What is an alloy?

☐ A type of pure substance

☐ A mixture of two or more metals

☐ A mixture of a solid and a liquid

☐ A chemical reaction

7.12) Which of these is a characteristic of a pure substance?

☐ It can be easily separated into other substances

☐ It has varying properties

☐ It consists of a single type of particle

☐ It is always a liquid

7.13) What is the main difference between a homogeneous and a heterogeneous mixture?

☐ The size of particles

☐ The ability to see the different parts

☐ The density of components

☐ The chemical properties

7.14) In a solution, what happens to the particles of the solute?

☐ They change their chemical properties

☐ They become invisible

☐ They dissolve and spread out evenly throughout the solvent

☐ They float to the top

7.15) What is distillation primarily used for?

☐ Separating solids from liquids

☐ Mixing two liquids

☐ Separating liquids based on boiling points

☐ Creating chemical reactions

7.16) Why can't a compound be considered a mixture?

☐ Because it only contains one type of molecule

☐ Because it can be separated by physical means

☐ Because it is always in a liquid state

☐ Because it is made of atoms

7.17) What is a characteristic feature of a colloid?

☐ It settles upon standing

☐ It scatters light

☐ It is always opaque

☐ It cannot be separated

7.18) What type of mixture is smoke?

☐ Solution

☐ Colloid

☐ Suspension

☐ Compound

7.19) How do the properties of a mixture compare to its components?

☐ They are always completely different

☐ They are exactly the same

☐ They vary depending on temperature

☐ They retain the properties of the individual substances

7.20) Why is air considered a mixture?

☐ Because it is colorless

☐ Because it consists of different gases mixed together

☐ Because it has a constant composition

☐ Because it can be compressed

7.21) What does it mean when a substance is 'miscible'?

☐ It can be compressed into a smaller volume

☐ It can be mixed with another substance to form a solution

☐ It reacts chemically with another substance

☐ It cannot be dissolved in a solvent

7.22) What is the main characteristic of a suspension?

☐ It has particles that dissolve completely

☐ It separates into layers over time

☐ It is always a type of gas

☐ It cannot be filtered

7.23) What role does temperature play in dissolving a substance?

☐ It does not affect dissolving

☐ It can increase or decrease the rate of dissolving

☐ It only affects liquids

☐ It changes the color of the solution

7.24) What is filtration used for?

☐ To combine two liquids

☐ To heat a mixture

☐ To separate a solid from a liquid in a mixture

☐ To change the chemical composition of a mixture

7.25) How is a compound different from a mixture?

☐ A compound is always a liquid, while a mixture can be in any state

☐ A compound is made of atoms, a mixture is made of molecules

☐ A compound can be separated by physical means, a mixture cannot

☐ A compound has a chemical bond between its components, a mixture does not

7.26) What is the boiling point?

☐ The temperature at which a liquid turns into a solid

☐ The temperature at which a liquid turns into a gas

☐ The temperature at which a gas turns into a liquid

☐ The temperature at which a solid turns into a gas

7.27) Why is melting point important in identifying a substance?

☐ Because it is different for each solid substance

☐ Because it is the same for all substances

☐ Because it indicates how a substance reacts chemically

☐ Because it determines the color of the substance

ALEXANDER-GRACE EDUCATION

7.28) What is evaporation?

☐ The process of a liquid turning into a solid

☐ The process of a gas turning into a liquid

☐ The process of a liquid turning into a gas

☐ The process of a solid turning into a liquid

7.29) What happens in a chemical reaction?

☐ Physical properties of substances change

☐ Substances are mixed without changing their chemical properties

☐ New substances with different properties are formed

☐ Substances are separated into their original components

7.30) What is the difference between a physical change and a chemical change?

☐ A physical change alters the shape, a chemical change alters the color

☐ A physical change is reversible, a chemical change is not

☐ A physical change creates a new substance, a chemical change does not

☐ A physical change affects size, a chemical change affects weight

7.31) What is crystallization?

☐ The process of a gas turning into a solid

☐ The process of forming a crystal structure in a substance

☐ The process of a liquid turning into a gas

☐ The process of mixing two liquids

7.32) What is the role of a catalyst in a chemical reaction?

□ It slows down the reaction

□ It changes the color of the products

□ It increases the temperature of the reaction

□ It speeds up the reaction without being consumed

7.33) What is the difference between an element and a compound?

□ An element is a type of compound

□ A compound is made of only one kind of atom, while an element can have different kinds

□ An element is made of only one kind of atom, while a compound is made of two or more different kinds

□ There is no difference, they are the same

7.34) What does the pH scale measure?

□ The boiling point of a substance

□ The acidity or basicity of a substance

□ The density of a substance

□ The melting point of a substance

7.35) What is a reactant in a chemical reaction?

□ The product formed as a result of the reaction

□ The substance that remains unchanged

□ The substance that is used up in the reaction

□ The substance that initiates the reaction

ALEXANDER-GRACE EDUCATION

7.36) What are the common states of matter?

☐ Solid, liquid, gas, and plasma

☐ Solid, liquid, gas, and compound

☐ Solid, liquid, gas, and metal

☐ Solid, liquid, gas, and element

7.37) What is sublimation?

☐ The process of a solid turning directly into a gas

☐ The process of a gas turning directly into a solid

☐ The process of a liquid turning into a gas

☐ The process of a gas turning into a liquid

7.38) What is a heterogeneous mixture?

☐ A mixture where the components are evenly mixed

☐ A mixture where the different components can be easily seen and separated

☐ A mixture that is always a liquid

☐ A mixture that reacts chemically

7.39) What is the role of a solvent in a solution?

☐ To dissolve the solute

☐ To change the color of the solution

☐ To increase the temperature of the solution

☐ To act as a container for the solution

7.40) What happens when a substance undergoes a physical change?

☐ It changes its chemical structure

☐ It combines with another substance to form a new one

☐ It changes in form or appearance without changing its chemical composition

☐ It becomes a different element

Topic 7 – Answers

Question Number	Answer	Explanation
7.1	A substance made of only one kind of material	A pure substance is made up of only one type of material, not a mixture.
7.2	Yes, because it's made of different substances that are not chemically combined	Mixtures can be separated because the substances in them are not chemically joined together.
7.3	A mixture where one substance dissolves in another	A solution is a special kind of mixture where one substance is completely dissolved in another.
7.4	Gold	Gold is a pure substance because it's made of only one type of material.
7.5	The substances in a solution are evenly distributed and don't settle out	In a solution, the substances mix so well that they don't separate over time.
7.6	The liquid in which the solute is dissolved	In a solution, the solvent is the liquid that dissolves the other substance.
7.7	The substance that is dissolved in the solvent	The solute is the part of a solution that gets dissolved by the solvent.
7.8	A combination of two or more substances that are not chemically combined	A mixture is made when two or more substances are combined without forming a new substance.
7.9	The salt and water become a solution	When salt dissolves in water, they form a solution. The salt doesn't disappear; it's just really well mixed.
7.10	Yes, because they are not chemically combined	Mixtures can be separated back into their original substances because they don't chemically react with each other.
7.11	A mixture of two or more metals	An alloy is a special kind of mixture where different metals are combined together.
7.12	It consists of a single type of particle	A pure substance has only one type of particle in it, making it the same throughout.
7.13	The ability to see the different parts	In a homogeneous mixture, you can't see the different parts; in a heterogeneous mixture, you can.
7.14	They dissolve and spread out evenly throughout the solvent	In a solution, the solute particles spread out and dissolve evenly in the solvent.
7.15	Separating liquids based on boiling points	Distillation separates liquids by using their different boiling points.
7.16	Because it only contains one type of molecule	A compound is made of molecules that are chemically combined, so it's not a mixture.
7.17	It scatters light	A colloid is a mixture where tiny particles are spread out and scatter light, like milk.
7.18	Colloid	Smoke is a colloid, a type of mixture where small particles are suspended in another substance.

7.19	They retain the properties of the individual substances	In a mixture, the different substances keep their own properties.
7.20	Because it consists of different gases mixed together	Air is a mixture because it's made up of different types of gases combined together.
7.21	It can be mixed with another substance to form a solution	If a substance is miscible, it can mix well with another substance to form a solution.
7.22	It separates into layers over time	A suspension is a type of mixture where the particles will eventually settle down over time.
7.23	It can increase or decrease the rate of dissolving	Changing the temperature can make a substance dissolve faster or slower in a solution.
7.24	To separate a solid from a liquid in a mixture	Filtration is used to separate solid particles from a liquid in a mixture.
7.25	A compound has a chemical bond between its components, a mixture does not	Compounds have chemically bonded components, while mixtures just combine substances without bonding them.
7.26	The temperature at which a liquid turns into a gas	The boiling point is the temperature where a liquid changes into a gas.
7.27	Because it is different for each solid substance	Melting points are unique to each substance, so they help identify different solid materials.
7.28	The process of a liquid turning into a gas	Evaporation is when a liquid heats up and turns into a gas.
7.29	New substances with different properties are formed	In a chemical reaction, substances mix and create new substances with different properties.
7.30	A physical change is reversible, a chemical change is not	A physical change can be undone, like melting ice. A chemical change creates new substances that can't be changed back.
7.31	The process of forming a crystal structure in a substance	Crystallization is when a material forms a solid crystal structure.
7.32	It speeds up the reaction without being consumed	A catalyst makes a chemical reaction go faster, but it doesn't get used up in the reaction.
7.33	An element is made of only one kind of atom, while a compound is made of two or more different kinds	Elements are simple substances with one type of atom. Compounds have two or more different atoms bonded together.
7.34	The acidity or basicity of a substance	The pH scale measures how acidic or basic a substance is.
7.35	The substance that initiates the reaction	Reactants are the substances that start a chemical reaction.
7.36	Solid, liquid, gas, and plasma	Matter can be in these four states: solid, liquid, gas, and plasma (like lightning or stars).
7.37	The process of a solid turning directly into a gas	Sublimation is when a solid changes directly into a gas without becoming a liquid first, like dry ice.
7.38	A mixture where the different components can be easily seen and separated	In a heterogeneous mixture, you can see and separate the different parts, like a salad.
7.39	To dissolve the solute	The solvent in a solution is the part that dissolves the other substance (solute).
7.40	It changes in form or appearance without changing its chemical composition	A physical change affects the shape or appearance, but the substance stays the same, like breaking a piece of chalk.

Topic 8 – Wave Properties

8.1) What is a wave?

☐ A movement in water

☐ A disturbance that carries energy through matter or space

☐ A type of sound

☐ A kind of electrical current

8.2) What are the two main types of waves?

☐ Sound and light

☐ Transverse and longitudinal

☐ Water and sound

☐ Electrical and magnetic

8.3) What is wavelength?

☐ The time it takes for a wave to complete one cycle

☐ The distance between two crests or troughs of a wave

☐ The height of a wave

☐ The speed of a wave

8.4) What is amplitude?

☐ The distance a wave travels

☐ The time a wave lasts

☐ The height of a wave from its rest position

☐ The number of waves per second

8.5) What does frequency refer to in a wave?

☐ The color of the wave

☐ The speed of the wave

☐ The number of waves that pass a point in one second

☐ The direction of the wave

8.6) What is a transverse wave?

☐ A wave that moves parallel to the direction of the energy

☐ A wave where the particles vibrate back and forth along the path of the wave

☐ A wave that moves perpendicular to the direction of the energy

☐ A wave that can only travel through solid materials

8.7) What is a longitudinal wave?

☐ A wave that moves perpendicular to the direction of the energy

☐ A wave where the particles vibrate back and forth along the path of the wave

☐ A wave that moves in a circular motion

☐ A wave that can only travel through liquids

8.8) How does sound travel?

☐ Through light

☐ As a transverse wave

☐ In a straight line

☐ As a longitudinal wave

ALEXANDER-GRACE EDUCATION

8.9) What happens when a wave reflects?

☐ It speeds up

☐ It changes direction when it hits a surface

☐ It stops moving

☐ It splits into two waves

8.10) What is refraction?

☐ The bending of waves due to a change in speed

☐ The reflection of waves off a surface

☐ The absorption of waves by a material

☐ The splitting of waves into colors

8.11) What causes a wave to occur?

☐ The presence of light

☐ A disturbance in the medium

☐ The rotation of the Earth

☐ Gravity pulling on the medium

8.12) What is a medium in the context of waves?

☐ A tool used to measure waves

☐ A state of matter

☐ The substance or material through which a wave travels

☐ The highest point of a wave

8.13) Can sound waves travel through a vacuum?

☐ Yes, but very slowly

☐ No, they need a medium like air, liquids, or solids

☐ Only in space

☐ Yes, very quickly

8.14) What is the speed of sound?

☐ Slower in air than in water

☐ Depends on the medium through which it's traveling

☐ Constant in all media

☐ Faster than light

8.15) What does a high frequency of a wave indicate?

☐ The wave is very long

☐ The wave is very slow

☐ There are more waves in a given time period

☐ The wave is very loud

8.16) Why do we see lightning before we hear thunder?

☐ Because light travels faster than sound

☐ Because thunder is always delayed

☐ Because sound travels faster than light

☐ Because lightning is brighter than thunder is loud

8.17) What is an echo?

☐ The absorption of sound by objects

☐ A type of musical instrument

☐ A special type of wave

☐ The reflection of sound waves off a surface

8.18) Why can you hear sound louder through a solid than through air?

☐ Because solids can amplify sound

☐ Because sound doesn't travel through solids

☐ Because solids have more space for sound to travel

☐ Because sound waves travel faster and more efficiently through solids

8.19) What happens to the frequency of a wave when its wavelength increases?

☐ The frequency increases

☐ The frequency remains the same

☐ The frequency decreases

☐ It becomes a different kind of wave

8.20) What is the main difference between noise and music?

☐ Music is louder than noise

☐ Music has a regular pattern of sound waves, while noise does not

☐ Noise is always unpleasant, while music is not

☐ Noise is a type of music

ALEXANDER-GRACE EDUCATION

8.21) What is interference in terms of waves?

□ The combination of two or more waves overlapping each other

□ The bending of waves around an obstacle

□ The breaking of waves into smaller waves

□ The reflection of waves from a surface

8.22) What type of wave is a sound wave?

□ Electromagnetic

□ Longitudinal

□ Transverse

□ Surface

8.23) What is diffraction?

□ The reflection of waves from a surface

□ The spreading out of waves as they pass through an opening or around an obstacle

□ The bending of waves due to a change in speed

□ The increase in wave amplitude

8.24) How do humans use ultrasonic waves?

□ For medical imaging and cleaning

□ For cooking food

□ To generate electricity

□ In telescopes to see distant stars

8.25) What determines the pitch of a sound?

☐ The amplitude of the sound wave

☐ The wavelength of the sound wave

☐ The frequency of the sound wave

☐ The color of the sound wave

8.26) What is the Doppler effect?

☐ The decrease in wave frequency as it moves away from the source

☐ The reflection of sound waves from a moving object

☐ The change in frequency of a wave in relation to an observer who is moving relative to the wave source

☐ The increase in wave speed as it moves away from the source

8.27) Why do we see different colors?

☐ Because light waves travel at different speeds

☐ Because of the different amplitudes of light waves

☐ Because of the different sizes of light waves

☐ Because of the different frequencies of light waves

8.28) What happens when light waves bend?

☐ They produce heat

☐ They create electricity

☐ This is known as refraction

☐ They become sound waves

8.29) Can waves transfer energy without transferring matter?

☐ No, they always transfer matter

☐ Only in a vacuum

☐ Yes, they can transfer energy without moving matter with them

☐ Only in water

8.30) What is a prism used for in terms of light waves?

☐ To break light into its component colors

☐ To increase the speed of light

☐ To generate light

☐ To reflect light

8.31) What is the purpose of a lens in relation to light waves?

☐ To change the direction of light waves

☐ To slow down the light waves

☐ To create new light waves

☐ To absorb light waves

8.32) What are seismic waves?

☐ Waves created by strong winds

☐ Sound waves in the ocean

☐ Light waves from the sun

☐ Waves caused by earthquakes that travel through Earth

8.33) What causes tides in the oceans?

☐ Changes in the Earth's temperature

☐ The movement of ships

☐ The gravitational pull of the moon and sun

☐ Wind over the ocean surface

8.34) What is the main source of electromagnetic waves?

☐ Artificial light sources

☐ The moon

☐ The sun

☐ The Earth's core

8.35) How does a microwave oven use waves?

☐ By using light waves to cook food

☐ By using microwaves to cause water molecules in food to vibrate and heat up

☐ By using seismic waves to shake food

☐ By using sound waves to heat food

8.36) What is the purpose of sunglasses in terms of waves?

☐ To help see sound waves

☐ To protect eyes from harmful ultraviolet (UV) waves

☐ To increase the brightness of light

☐ To change the color of light

8.37) How do radio waves transmit information?

☐ By carrying sound only

☐ By altering their frequency to carry signals

☐ By changing their speed

☐ By reflecting off objects

8.38) What is visible light?

☐ A wave that is always invisible

☐ The only type of light wave that exists

☐ A type of sound wave

☐ Light that can be seen by the human eye

8.39) Why can we hear sound better in water than in air?

☐ Because sound waves travel faster and more efficiently in water

☐ Because air absorbs sound

☐ Because water conducts electricity better

☐ Because water amplifies sound

8.40) What are gamma rays?

☐ A type of sound wave

☐ The longest waves in the electromagnetic spectrum

☐ Waves that can only be found in space

☐ High-energy waves used in medical imaging

ALEXANDER-GRACE EDUCATION

Topic 8 – Answers

Question Number	Answer	Explanation
8.1	A disturbance that carries energy through matter or space	Waves are not just in water; they are disturbances that move energy, like sound or light waves.
8.2	Transverse and longitudinal	Waves can be transverse (moving up and down) or longitudinal (moving back and forth).
8.3	The distance between two crests or troughs of a wave	Wavelength is how far apart the highest or lowest parts of a wave are.
8.4	The height of a wave from its rest position	Amplitude is how tall a wave is from its normal, flat state.
8.5	The number of waves that pass a point in one second	Frequency tells us how many waves go by a point in one second.
8.6	A wave that moves perpendicular to the direction of the energy	In transverse waves, the movement is up and down compared to the direction the wave travels.
8.7	A wave where the particles vibrate back and forth along the path of the wave	In longitudinal waves, particles move back and forth in the same direction as the wave.
8.8	As a longitudinal wave	Sound travels as a longitudinal wave, with vibrations in the same direction as the wave moves.
8.9	It changes direction when it hits a surface	When a wave reflects, it bounces off a surface and goes in a new direction.
8.10	The bending of waves due to a change in speed	Refraction is when waves bend because they're moving faster or slower in a new medium.
8.11	A disturbance in the medium	Waves happen because something disturbs or shakes up the medium (like air, water, or ground).
8.12	The substance or material through which a wave travels	A medium is what the wave travels through, like air for sound waves or water for ocean waves.
8.13	No, they need a medium like air, liquids, or solids	Sound waves can't travel through a vacuum; they need something to move through.
8.14	Depends on the medium through which it's traveling	Sound moves at different speeds in different materials, like faster in water than in air.
8.15	There are more waves in a given time period	High frequency means a wave has many cycles in a short time.
8.16	Because light travels faster than sound	We see lightning before we hear thunder because light reaches us faster than sound.
8.17	The reflection of sound waves off a surface	An echo is when sound waves bounce off a surface and come back to us.
8.18	Because sound waves travel faster and more efficiently through solids	Sound can move better through solids than air because the particles are closer together.
8.19	The frequency decreases	When the wavelength gets longer, the frequency (how many waves per second) goes down.

8.20	Music has a regular pattern of sound waves, while noise does not	Music is organized sound, while noise is random sounds without a pattern.
8.21	The combination of two or more waves overlapping each other	Interference happens when waves meet and overlap, creating a new wave pattern.
8.22	Longitudinal	Sound waves are longitudinal because their particles move back and forth in the same direction as the wave.
8.23	The spreading out of waves as they pass through an opening or around an obstacle	Diffraction is when waves spread out after passing through a gap or around an edge.
8.24	For medical imaging and cleaning	Ultrasonic waves are used in things like ultrasound to see inside the body or to clean things deeply.
8.25	The frequency of the sound wave	Pitch in sound depends on the frequency; high frequency is a high pitch, and low frequency is a low pitch.
8.26	The change in frequency of a wave in relation to an observer who is moving relative to the wave source	The Doppler effect is why a siren sounds different as it moves towards you and then away from you.
8.27	Because of the different frequencies of light waves	We see colors differently because each color of light has a different frequency.
8.28	This is known as refraction	When light waves bend, it's called refraction, like when a straw looks bent in water.
8.29	Yes, they can transfer energy without moving matter with them	Waves like light or radio waves can move energy without carrying matter along.
8.30	To break light into its component colors	A prism can split white light into a rainbow of colors.
8.31	To change the direction of light waves	Lenses bend light waves to focus or spread them out, like in glasses or cameras.
8.32	Waves caused by earthquakes that travel through Earth	Seismic waves are created by earthquakes and can travel through the Earth.
8.33	The gravitational pull of the moon and sun	Tides are caused by the gravitational pull of the moon and sun on Earth's oceans.
8.34	The sun	The sun is a major source of electromagnetic waves, like light.
8.35	By using microwaves to cause water molecules in food to vibrate and heat up	Microwaves in an oven make water in food heat up, cooking the food.
8.36	To protect eyes from harmful ultraviolet (UV) waves	Sunglasses block UV light from the sun, which can be harmful to our eyes.
8.37	By altering their frequency to carry signals	Radio waves carry information by changing their frequency.
8.38	Light that can be seen by the human eye	Visible light is the part of light waves that our eyes can see.
8.39	Because sound waves travel faster and more efficiently in water	Sound is clearer in water because it travels better through the denser medium.
8.40	High-energy waves used in medical imaging	Gamma rays are very high-energy waves used in things like cancer treatment.

Ready for More?

The NWEA MAP testing is adaptive. This means that if your student found these questions too tricky or too easy, they may find it useful to practice grades below or above they grade they are in. This will expose students to new concepts and ideas, giving them a better chance at scoring higher in tests.

Alexander-Grace Education produces books covering Mathematics, Sciences, and English, to help your student maximize their potential in these areas.

For errata, please email
alexandergraceeducation@gmail.com

ALEXANDER-GRACE EDUCATION

Made in United States
Orlando, FL
11 September 2024

51407447R00059